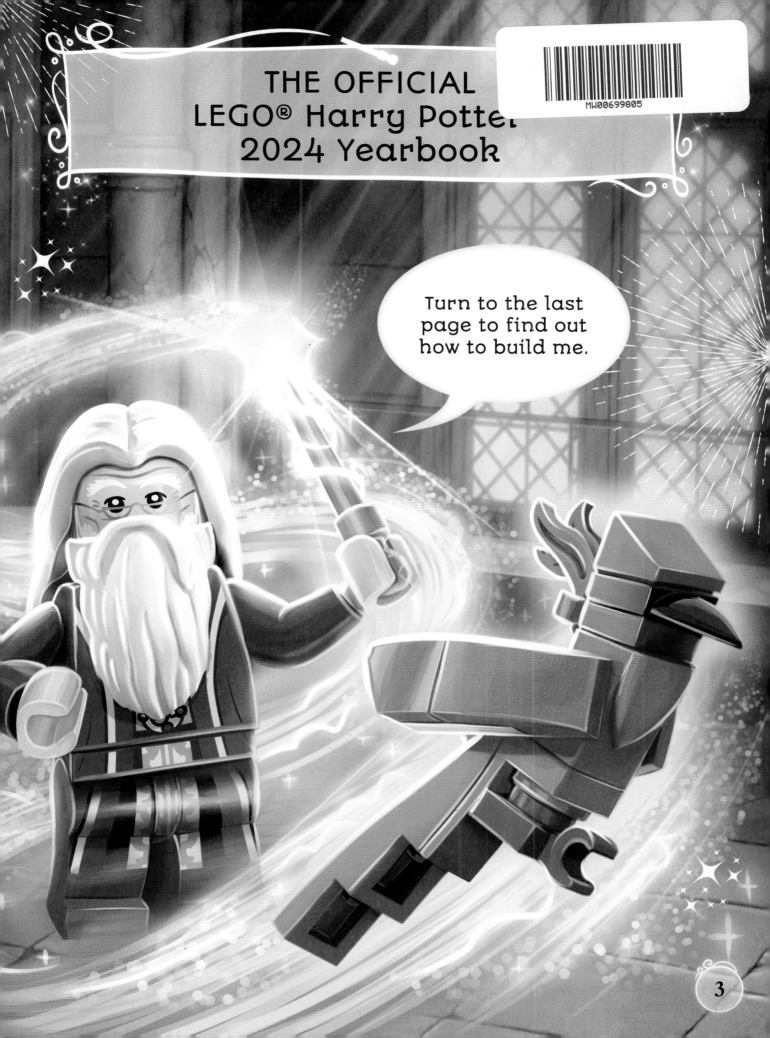

THE OFFICIAL LEGO® Harry Potter 2024 Yearbook

Turn to the last page to find out how to build me.

Get to know ...
Professor Albus Dumbledore

Hogwarts history:
Former student and current
Headmaster of Hogwarts
School of Witchcraft and
Wizardry

Likes:
Warm woolly socks

Dislikes:
Bertie Bott's Every Flavour
Beans ... earwax flavour

Known for:
Being the greatest
wizard of his time

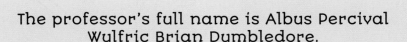
The professor's full name is Albus Percival
Wulfric Brian Dumbledore.

Professor Dumbledore has an unusual animal companion: a phoenix named Fawkes!

During the First Wizarding War, Dumbledore founded a secret society of witches and wizards to fight Lord Voldemort. Together, they're known as the Order of the Phoenix.

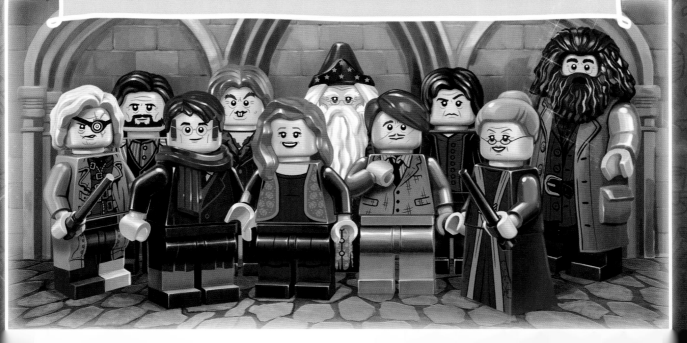

Professor Dumbledore must hide Hagrid and little Harry from Muggles' prying eyes. Find a route that allows him to put out all the lamps without retracing his steps.

FINISH

START

Dumbledore says something to little Harry before he leaves him with the Dursleys. To discover what he said, find the cloud that is identical to the one next to Dumbledore.

Goodbye, Harry Potter.

You are the Boy Who Lived.

I will return.

Good luck, Harry Potter.

Harry got the Dumbledore collectable card in his first ever Chocolate Frog box! Can you find the Dumbledore card that is different from the others?

1

2

3

4

5

6

I got Dumbledore!

7

Dumbledore introduces the students to the Hogwarts professors. Can you match the professors to their shadows?

Welcome to another year at Hogwarts.

The Mirror of Erised shows the heart's deepest desires. What does Dumbledore believe he will see in it? Find out by matching the shape with the one on the mirror.

Can you draw a portrait of Albus Dumbledore?
It's easy! You can learn it in four simple steps.

It's time for Dumbledore to present the House Cup. To find out who wins it, match the crests to the animal shapes.

Which house will triumph?

1 HUFFLEPUFF
2 RAVENCLAW
3 GRYFFINDOR
4 SLYTHERIN

1st
482 points

2nd
472 points

3rd
426 points

4th
352 points

Dumbledore has borrowed Fluffy, a huge, three-headed dog, from Hagrid. Find out what Fluffy is guarding by working out which item has no matching pair.

Dumbledore's faithful companion, Fawkes, is a phoenix who can be reborn by rising from ashes. Find the group of parts that belong to Fawkes so he can come back to life.

1

2

Fascinating creatures, phoenixes.

3

Harry often visits Dumbledore's office. Can you find the 10 differences between these two pictures of his latest visit?

Draw straight lines to connect the matching pairs of symbols. The professor left with no line crossing through them is the one who Harry thinks is the greatest sorcerer in the world.

Use the coloured dots as your guide to colour in this picture of Fawkes as a baby.

Help Fawkes find his way to Harry, so he can help him in the Chamber of Secrets.

START

FINISH

Connect the dots to see the monster that Harry and Fawkes battle in the Chamber of Secrets.

What saves Harry from the Basilisk's venom?
To find out, find the item with the symbols that match the order of the symbols in the box.

1 The Grey Lady's diadem

2 The tears of a phoenix

3 Chocolate Frogs

4 The Golden Snitch

Professor Dumbledore has cancelled all exams! Celebrate the good news by finding each of the circled pictures in the main scene. One has been found for you.

Harry has been attacked by Dementors! Put a cross in the circle next to the spell that matches the colour code below to find out what Dumbledore says to save him.

○ Vera Verto

○ Arresto Momentum

○ Bombarda Maxima

○ Episkey

Hermione and Harry used a Time-Turner to go back in time and save Sirius Black. Can you find the real Time-Turner? It is the one that's different from the rest.

Three turns should do it, I think.

Thanks to Hermione and Harry, Sirius has managed to escape and avoid returning to Azkaban. Can you find each of the picture boxes in the main scene? One has been found for you.

Dumbledore shows Harry a cabinet filled with glittering vials. How many vials can you count?

Each vial holds a memory, but whose memory is it? Work out which vial matches the one in the box to find out.

Colour the vials in the same order that the coloured drops are falling into them.

What you are looking at are memories.

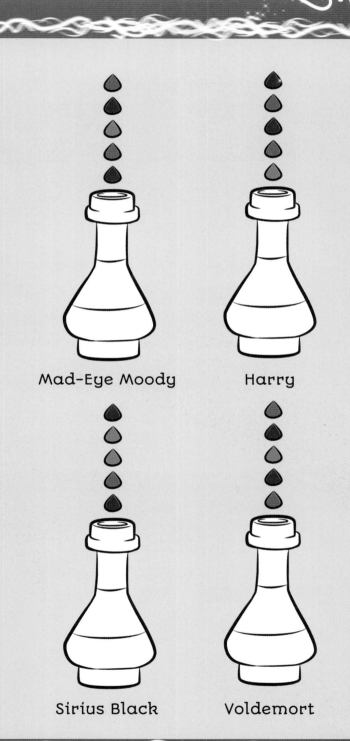

Mad-Eye Moody

Harry

Sirius Black

Voldemort

19

Professor Slughorn has used a spell to disguise himself as an armchair! Can you number the jumbled picture pieces correctly?

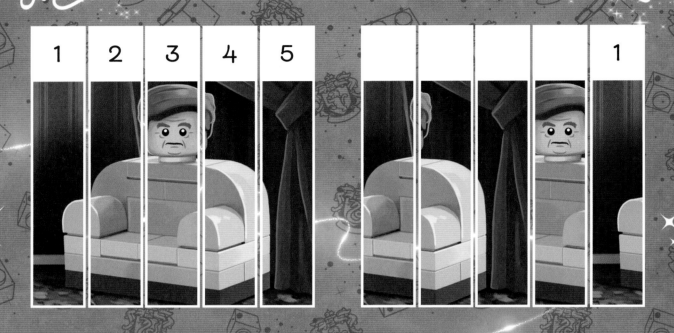

Find each of the picture combinations on the left and draw around them in the grid on the right. The person left at the end is the one who Dumbledore wants to see in Professor Slughorn's memory. One has been done for you.

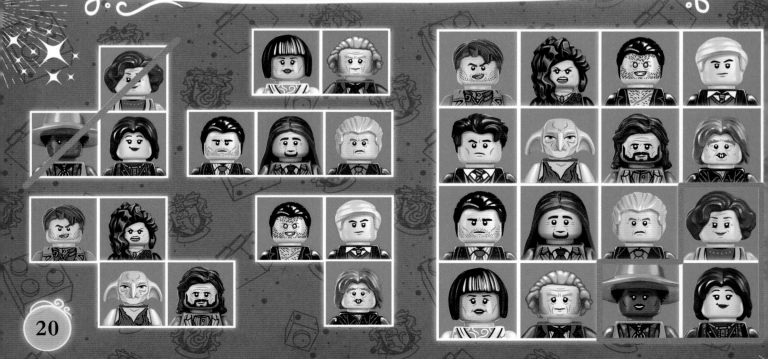

Dumbledore belonged to Gryffindor when he was a Hogwarts student. Look at the 10 items shown below and see if you can find them in the Gryffindor common room.

Use the clues to help Dumbledore find out who put Harry's name into the Goblet of Fire. When you've found who it is, put a cross in the circle next to them.

They are not wearing a hat.

********∞∞∞∞********

They do not have red hair.

********∞∞∞∞********

They are wearing a brown jacket.

For the first task in the Triwizard Tournament, Harry has to battle a dangerous Hungarian Horntail Dragon! Use the code shown on the left to colour in this frightening creature.

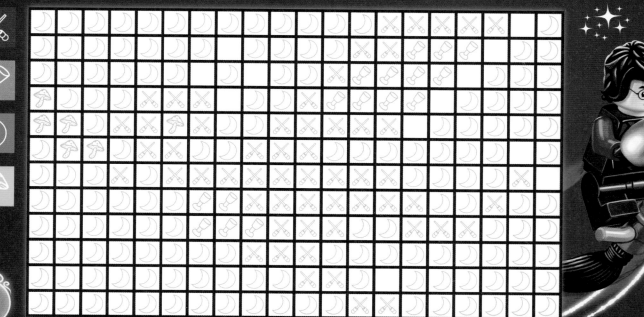

Viktor, Harry, Cedric and Fleur are searching for their friends at the bottom of the lake. Match their colour codes to find out who saves who.

What does Viktor Krum transfigure his head into during the second Triwizard Tournament task? Find the arrow pattern matching the one in the box to find out, then put a cross in the circle next to that character.

Dumbledore is good friends with Mad-Eye Moody. Who does Mad-Eye have his magical eye on?

Dumbledore has shown up at the Ministry of Magic to help a group of students. Work out who is missing from each row and write their letters in the empty circles.

Voldemort unleashes fire, but Dumbledore creates a ball of water to keep Harry safe. Help him by matching the puzzle pieces to the empty spaces in the picture.

Voldemort tries to steal something from the Ministry of Magic. Use the colour code to work your way through the objects and find out what it was.

START   COLOUR CODE

Dumbledore's friends gather for the Order of the Phoenix secret meeting. Look at the characters below each picture. Cross out the one missing from each scene to find out who has not arrived yet.

1

2

3

4

Use the symbol codes to match the witches
and wizards to their objects.

1

2

3

4

5

28

Draw an expression on Harry's face to show his reaction to each thing that has happened to him.

Drinking the disgusting Polyjuice Potion.

Duelling with Lord Voldemort.

Gryffindor winning the Quidditch game.

Oh no! The Ministry has come to take Dumbledore to Azkaban. Help him escape by finding a path that only contains pictures of Fawkes.

START →

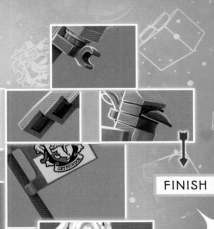

FINISH

Dumbledore's friend Professor Lupin changes into a werewolf during every full moon. Put the pictures in order by numbering each stage of his transformation from human to werewolf. The first one has been done for you.

1

Dumbledore has left Harry the Golden Snitch as a reward for his perseverance and skill. Find the Snitch that matches the big one.

You've reached the halfway point of this magical adventure. Answer these questions and find out how well you know Professor Dumbledore.

1 Professor Dumbledore's first name is:

A Albus

B Sirius

C Cedric

2 What is Dumbledore's role at Hogwarts?

A Gamekeeper

B Headmaster

C Professor of Defence Against the Dark Arts

3 Who is Dumbledore's companion?

A   B   C

4 What kind of glasses does Dumbledore wear?

A   B   C

5 What did Professor Dumbledore create?

A Quidditch

B The Order of the Phoenix

C The Goblet of Fire

Get to know ...
Lord Voldemort

Hogwarts history:
Former student and
Slytherin Prefect

Likes:
His followers, the Death Eaters

Dislikes:
Muggles

Known for:
Being the most powerful
Dark wizard and speaking
Parseltongue

Lord Voldemort's real name is Tom Marvolo Riddle.

32

He is the heir of Salazar Slytherin, one of the founders of Hogwarts.

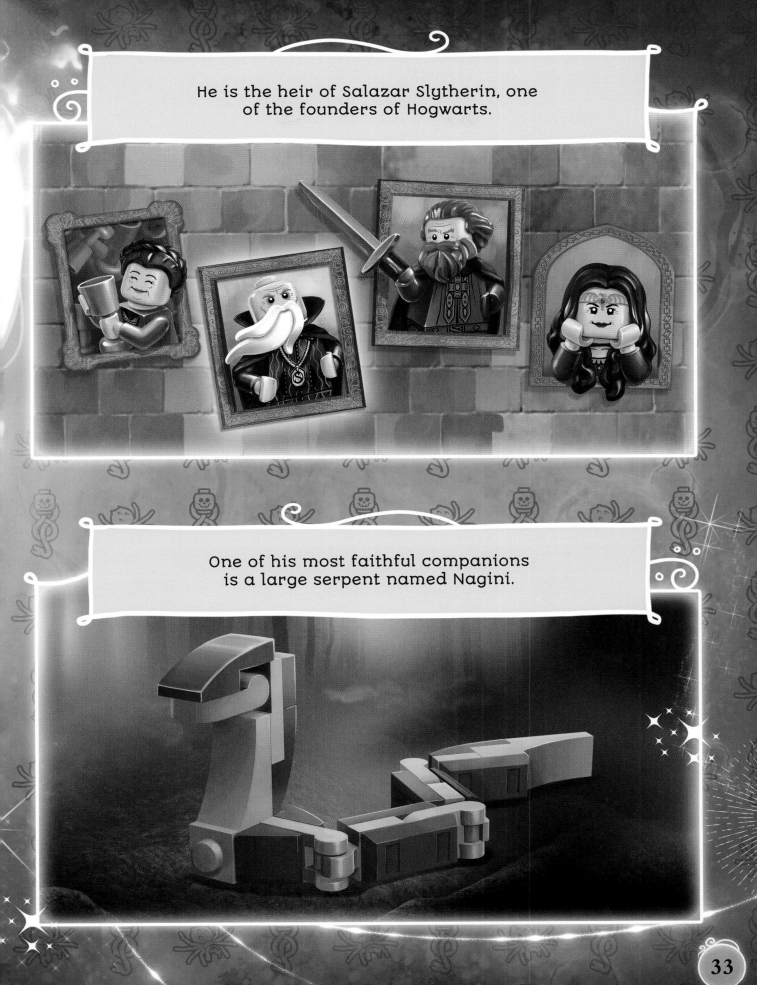

One of his most faithful companions is a large serpent named Nagini.

Tom Riddle was a member of Slytherin House. Look closely at what's happening in the Slytherin common room and mark 10 differences between the pictures.

Find the coordinates listed in the white box and cross them out. The person who remains is the one who Harry suspected of being the heir of Slytherin. One has been crossed out for you.

B1 A2 C1
A1 C2

Nagini is Voldemort's faithful snake companion. Can you number the jumbled picture pieces correctly?

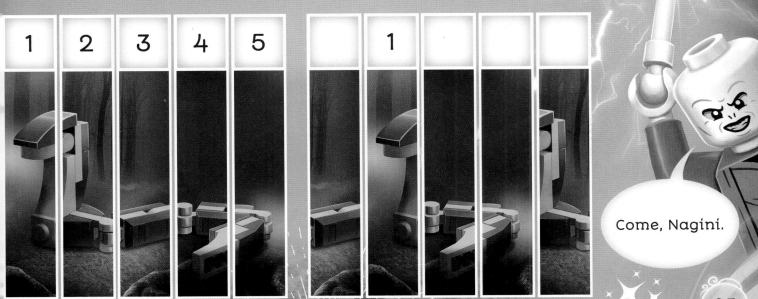

Come, Nagini.

35

Many wizards and witches support Voldemort. Can you spot which of the silhouettes matches the picture of this terrifying group?

A

B

D

C

One object has the power to destroy Tom Riddle's diary. To find it, look for the object inside the cloud that matches the empty cloud next to Tom.

A huge statue of Salazar Slytherin adorns the Chamber of Secrets. Use the grid and copy the left-hand side of the picture to complete this drawing of the statue.

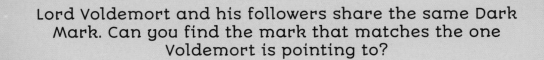

Lord Voldemort and his followers share the same Dark Mark. Can you find the mark that matches the one Voldemort is pointing to?

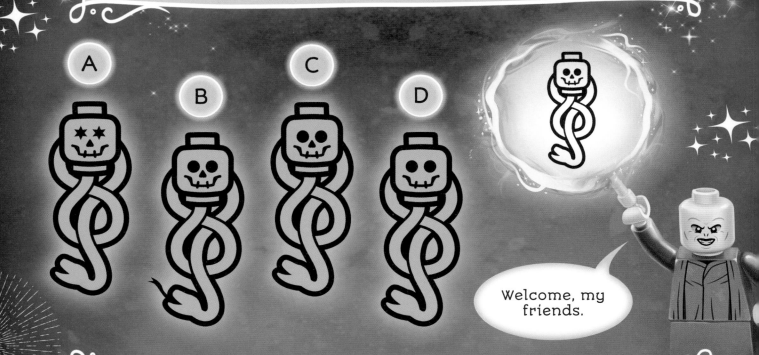

A B C D

Welcome, my friends.

What animal does Wormtail, Voldemort's henchman, transform into to hide from everyone? Use a grey pen or pencil and colour in the areas marked with a star shape to find out.

38

Find the path that leads to Harry to reveal who helps him to safety when Voldemort challenges him to a duel.

Find the arrow pattern matching the one in the white box to find out who Barty Crouch Jr. changes into after drinking Polyjuice Potion.

Find the character on the right who appears in all four of these groups to discover who falls under Voldemort's evil spell in the Chamber of Secrets.

One of the students starts to work for Lord Voldemort. To find out who it is, look for the student who appears only once in the grid.

Which professor works for Voldemort? Find out by drawing around the character combinations below and seeing who is left. One has been done for you.

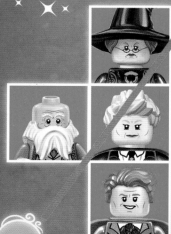

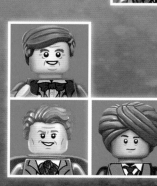

What is Harry giving to Dobby? Work out which torn picture piece is the correct one and all will be revealed.

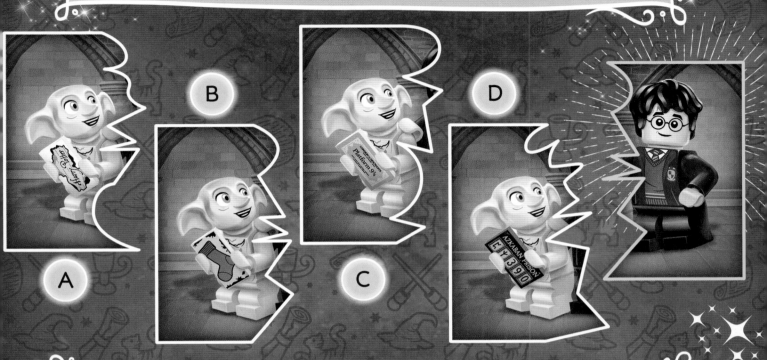

B

D

A

C

Harry has been attacked by Dementors on the Hogwarts Express! Can you spot where the six picture pieces appear in the scene? One has been found for you.

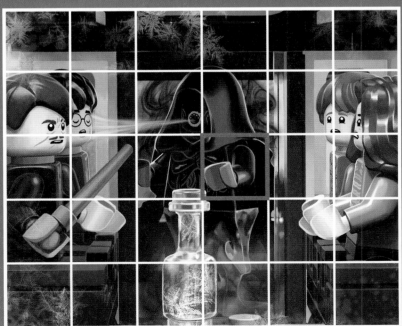

43

Before Voldemort became a powerful Dark wizard, he was a regular student. Put the pictures in order by numbering each stage of his transformation from Tom Riddle to Lord Voldemort. The first number has been added for you.

1

Ron has swallowed poison! Help Harry find the antidote by working out which jigsaw piece fits in the picture.

A

B

C

D

E

F

This is the Shrieking Shack. Look at each group of parts and work out which part from each group belongs to the house. The first one has been done for you.

Harry and his school friends have formed Dumbledore's Army. Fill in the numbers of the students who should appear in each blank space. One has been done for you.

Voldemort's accomplices want to discredit Harry in the
Daily Prophet. Count how many newspapers there are
and write the total in the white box.

Connect the dots to find out what protects Dolores
Umbridge from the Dementors in the Ministry of Magic.

Voldemort needs to borrow a wand from one of his allies.
Use the clues from the box to find out who it is.

They are holding
something.

They have
long hair.

They wear
a black robe.

Voldemort thinks he has the Elder Wand, but he doesn't. To
find out who really has it, find the person below who is not
pointed to by any of the wands. Note that wands can point
at more than one person.

Voldemort is the most powerful Dark wizard!
Use the following steps to draw him.

Horcruxes achieve immortality by splitting a Dark wizard's soul into separate pieces. Find the path below that will pick up all the Horcruxes before Voldemort gets to them.

I read something rather odd about a bit of rare magic.

A   B   C   D

Marvolo Gaunt's ring is one of the first Horcruxes.
Find the character whose symbols match the code
to learn who discovers the ring.

1 **Severus Snape**

2 **Harry Potter**

3 **Albus Dumbledore**

4 **Neville Longbottom**

Harry, Ron and Hermione have taken Slytherin's locket
from Umbridge. Use the coloured dots to colour in the
picture and find out what the locket looks like.

Who is helping Harry to find Rowena Ravenclaw's diadem?
Match the character to the silhouette to find out.

Find the path that matches the symbols in the white box
to lead Harry to the diadem so he can destroy it.

The Room of Requirement is filled with many treasures. Can you find all eight objects from the white box in this busy scene?

Which of the below items does Neville use to stop Nagini's attack? It's the one that has no matching pair.

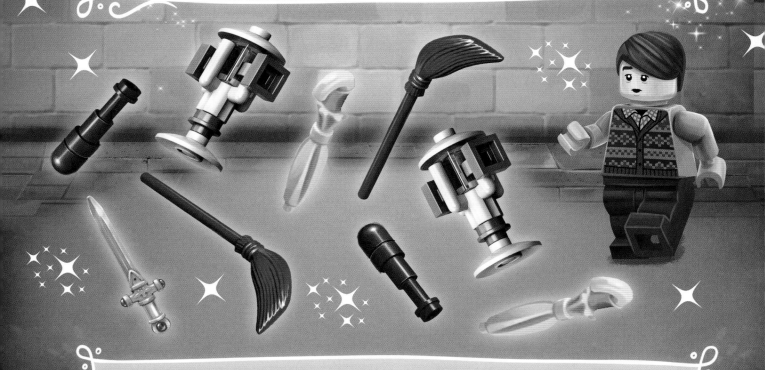

Find the line that leads to Harry to discover who betrays him during the Hogwarts war with Voldemort.

Harry and Voldemort are duelling in the Hogwarts courtyard. Can you find the 10 differences between these two action-packed scenes?

Harry has saved Hogwarts! Help him rebuild it by putting the jigsaw pieces in the right places.

1

2

3

4

5

6

You've reached the end of this magical adventure.
Answer these questions to find out how well you
know the Dark Lord.

1

Lord Voldemort's real name is:

A Sirius Black

B Severus Snape

C Tom Marvolo Riddle

2

Voldemort is heir of which
Hogwarts House?

A   B   C

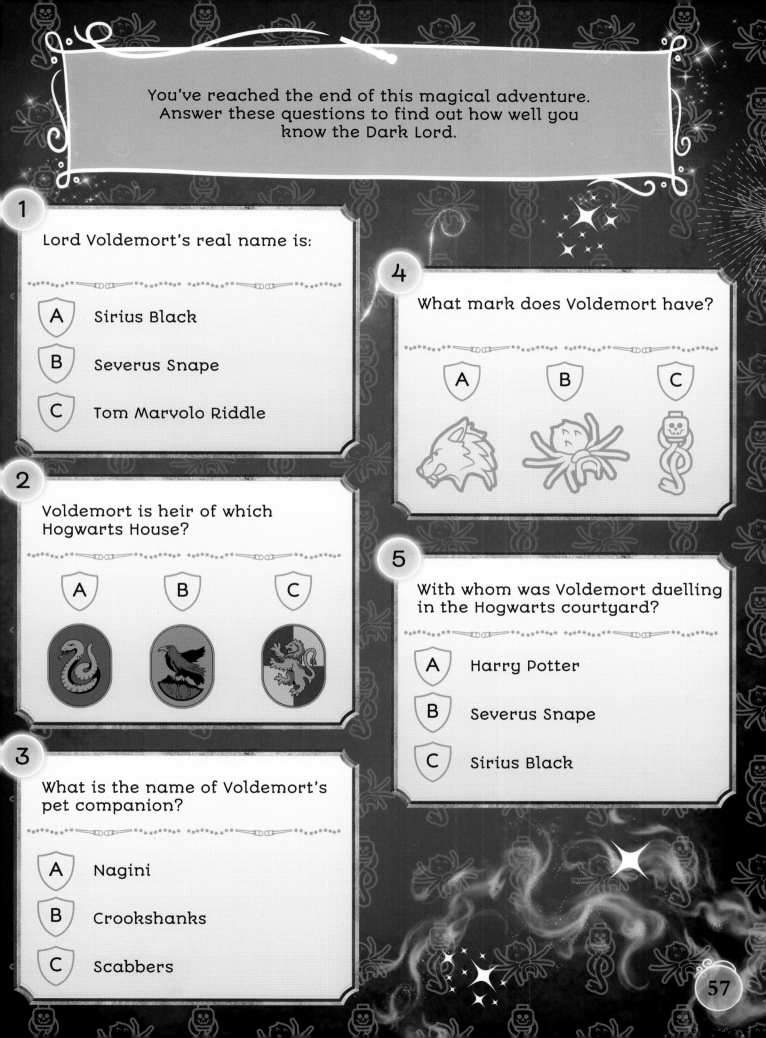

3

What is the name of Voldemort's
pet companion?

A Nagini

B Crookshanks

C Scabbers

4

What mark does Voldemort have?

A   B   C

5

With whom was Voldemort duelling
in the Hogwarts courtyard?

A Harry Potter

B Severus Snape

C Sirius Black

ANSWERS

p. 6

p. 7

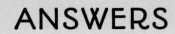

Good luck, Harry Potter.

5

p. 8

3 5 6

1

2 4

p. 10

1st	2nd
482 points	472 points
3	4

3rd	4th
426 points	352 points
2	1

p. 11

2

p. 12

p. 13

p. 14

p. 15

2

The tears of a phoenix

p. 16

p. 17

Arresto Momentum

p. 18

= 9

p. 19

Voldemort

p. 20

2	4	5	3	1

p. 21

58

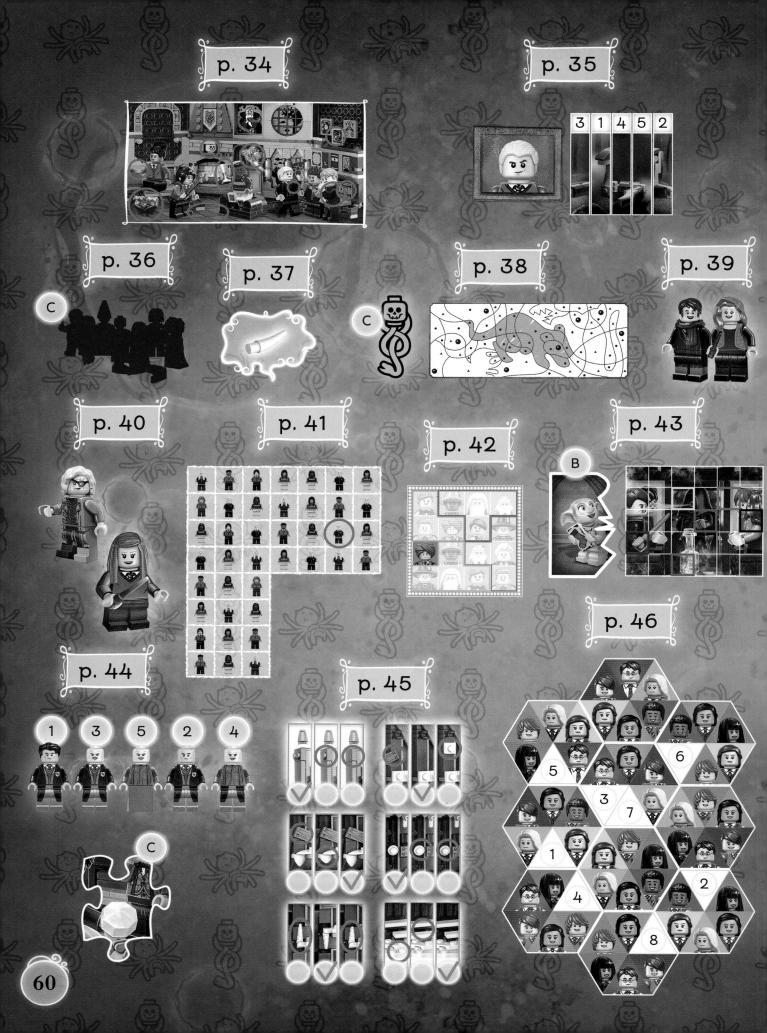

p. 47

= 8

p. 48

p. 50

C

p. 52

C

p. 53

p. 51

3

Albus Dumbledore

p. 54

p. 55

p. 56

3

5

2

1

4

6

p. 57

How to build
Albus Dumbledore